AF382677

HOW TO WRITE A SUCCESSFUL COVER LETTER

Ace your application

Written by Benoit Janssens
Translated by Ciaran Traynor

Coaching 50MINUTES.com

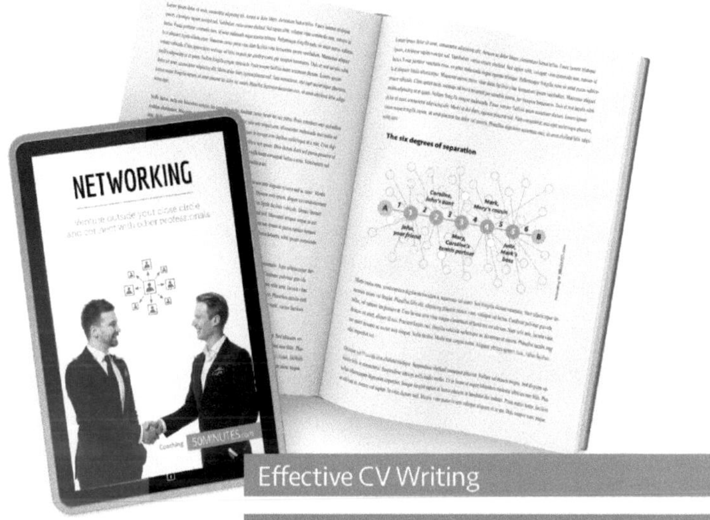

HOW TO WRITE A SUCCESSFUL COVER LETTER

- **Problem**: how can you write a cover letter that will get you an interview?
- **Uses**: a cover letter complements and enhances your CV. It allows the candidate to emphasise some of their strengths more than others to fit the job they are applying for, and it also gives the employer an overall view of the candidate's profile, personality, experiences, skills and motivation.
- **Professional context**: job or internship searching, career change.
- **FAQs**:
  - What makes an emailed cover letter different one sent by post?
  - Is it a good idea to handwrite your cover letter?
  - Should you always send a cover letter with your CV?

- What arguments should you make when you have little or no professional experience?
- Can you add a touch of humour to your cover letter?
- How can you appear enthusiastic without coming across as arrogant?
- Can you use the same cover letter for every job?
- Should you mention the distance between the workplace and home?

Have you just graduated, lost your job or decided that you want to change careers? Well, unless you plan on setting up your own business, you are going to have to apply for a job or an internship. You now have to think about writing a cover letter, which is almost always expected for job applications.

In fact, no matter your professional situation and the job you want to apply for, a cover letter is crucial. It is usually the second document read by the recruiter, after your CV. Your chances of being hired therefore depend greatly on the quality and coherence of this letter.

However, do not forget that, even if your cover letter is beautifully written and perfectly matches the job description, this is not a guarantee of success. No matter how many strengths and how much motivation you manage to convey with your cover letter, the employer might simply prefer another candidate's CV. Not only that, there are other important stages which you still have to get through, particularly the interview(s). That being said, in order to have the opportunity to get to this point, you have no choice but to spend some time on this first, decisive step: your cover letter.

This can be quite the challenge if you have never written one before. Even worse, you may think you know how to write a good cover letter, but you keep getting turned down. If this sounds like you, it may be time to rethink your approach in order to write the best letter possible.

But where to begin? What are the most important elements to include to make your application more convincing? Never fear, this practical little guide will give you all the help you need to find the job of your dreams!

A CONVINCING COVER LETTER: THE BASICS

A NECESSARY STAGE

For the candidate

In a nutshell, a cover letter shows why you want the job. It is different from your CV, which is more a summary of your professional career and your skills. Therefore, do not simply repeat what you have already said in your CV in slightly different words: on no account should the two documents be identical. That does not mean that you cannot mention the same sort of things, however. Although putting across your skills and experience is the domain of your CV, your cover letter can allow you to concisely develop the main points and justify why you want the job. It allow you to link some of your qualities and skills with certain memorable experiences from your career. However, be careful not to turn your cover letter into an autobiography!

Before applying for a job, it goes without saying that you have to be sure that you have the right qualifications. Motivation alone is not enough. You will only have a chance of interesting the employer if you demonstrate that you both qualify for the job (through your CV) and are motivated to get it (through your cover letter). It is therefore essential to read the job advert carefully before you begin writing your cover letter.

However, you do not need to satisfy all the criteria in the job application. Recruiters advertise for their ideal candidate. Some of the things they are looking for are obligatory, and will be clearly stated as such (for example, a "category B driving licence" or a certain level of education). However, your motivation can compensate for one or two skills that you do not yet have. So try not to throw in the towel too soon: it would be a shame to let an opportunity pass you by because you lack one little element that the employer wants, even though apart from that you may be ideal for the job.

For the recruiter

Most employers receive dozens, even hundreds of job applications for every position. Interviewing all the candidates would be a waste of time and money. The CV and the cover letter therefore allow them to narrow down their choice.

In most cases, the CV is the first document that the recruiter is interested in. If it makes them think that your profile corresponds more or less to what they are looking for, they will move on to your cover letter. Since it is the second thing they read, your cover letter should therefore not be overlooked. It is a "plus" which can make you stand out from the other candidates. You may have a good CV, but a poorly written cover letter can spell the end of your application.

However, the recruitment procedure does not always happen like this. Your cover letter may be the first thing the recruiter reads. In this case, it becomes even more important. If it does not impress the recruiter, there is a good chance that they will not even take the time to look at your CV.

Analyse the job advert in detail

As we have already seen, the first step is to assure yourself that you have understood and assimilated the essentials of the job you are applying for. Take some time to analyse the advertisement in detail. This should already give you an idea of what to focus on when you write your cover letter. Try to match each of the employer's requirements to a skill or experience.

Next, try to work out which of your qualities will be the most useful for the job. Employers generally provide a job description as well a list of necessary qualifications and required qualities. As a simple example, if it is indicated that the employee will have to interact with colleagues on a daily basis, it would be a good idea to mention that you enjoy teamwork, even if this characteristic is not explicitly asked for.

Job adverts are sometimes not very detailed and can be a bit unclear regarding the position and what it actually involves. In this case, do not hesitate to contact the person in charge of recruitment by email or phone for more information. However, try not to do this if you do not have any specific questions to ask.

Once you are sure that your application is coherent and suits the profile the employer is looking for, you can move on to the next step.

Find out as much as you can about the employer and the industry

In order to understand who you are dealing with, find out everything you can about the employer. There are several ways of doing this.

- Internet: Employers, no matter who they are, tend to have a website. You can find useful information about the position of the business in its industry, its philosophy, how it works, how important it is compared to potential rivals, its history, and so on.

- Social networking: check if the employer has a social media page (mainly on Facebook or LinkedIn). If so, you may be able to find out information about their popularity, their brand image and their activities.
- Your own network: it is always a good idea to ask people you know about the job or the employer. Who knows, somebody might be familiar with the company or someone who works there.
- The press: if you are applying to a big company, you can also find out information from the general or financial press. The employer may have been or be in the news.
- Telephone: the employer's phone number can almost always be found in the job advert. Employers often even encourage candidates to call them to find out more about the job. Even if you just have questions about the company, do not be afraid to give them a quick call, after checking that you cannot find the information using the means described above, of course. Even if the job advert does not encourage you to phone them, you have nothing to lose by trying your luck. On the contrary, this will

simply show the employer how interested and serious you are about the job. If you are not particularly comfortable talking on the phone, improvisation will not end well: try to note down what you want to ask beforehand.

SOME EXTRA ADVICE

If the name of the recruiter is featured in the job advert, try to find out what their role is in the company. This information will allow you to personalise your cover letter a bit more by addressing it to someone in particular. You can therefore begin the letter with something like "Dear Hiring Manager" instead of the simple "Dear Sir" or "Dear Madam", which will reinforce the impression that you are committed to getting the job.

If you are applying for a job in a sector that you are not very familiar with, it is also useful to find out more about it. For example, if you are applying to be a secretary in the industrial sector and you have only worked in the business sector, it is essential to know the differences between the two.

Why is all this information necessary?

All this research will allow you to better target the organisation you are applying to. This will not only help you to write your cover letter, but will also allow you to write a better CV and be more confident in potential interviews which may follow. Any further communication will be influenced by what you learn during your preliminary search for information.

To come back to the cover letter itself, it goes without saying that you have to adapt the subject of your application depending to the post you are applying to. However, this is not the only element that you have to think about. Indeed, both the tone you use and the strengths you highlight will depend on the employer. You can therefore increase your chances of success by adapting your cover letter to each employer. For example, your cover letter for a multinational company will obviously be different from the one you send to a small family business, even if you are applying for the same post. You will highlight different points, whether regarding your motivation or your strengths.

	Multinational company	**Small business**
Motivations	• Working in a prestigious company • Possibility of mobility within the enterprise (possibly even international mobility) • Working with large structures and teams	• Work in a company with a more human side to it • Possibility to move up quickly within the company • Greater responsibilities given the size of the company
Skills and qualities	• Autonomous • Discipline • Specialisation in a particular type of work	• Able to work in a team • Ability to take the initiative • Proactive

You may well have the qualities and motivation for the two companies but, depending on your employer, some will be more important than others.

IDENTIFY THE EMPLOYER'S PROFILE

There are a number of criteria which will allow you to differentiate between employers. Here is a non-exhaustive list:

- the size of the organisation,
- what it produces or creates (any kind of product or service),

- its reputation,
- its philosophy,
- its origin (nationality of the parent company),
- its history,
- its hierarchy,
- its reputation.

If you go about it this way, your cover letter will be unique and will therefore have a greater chance of attracting the attention of the person in charge of recruitment. Indeed, the difference between a generic letter that you copy and paste for each job and a personalised letter using the advice above is glaringly obvious. Tanguy V., a professional recruiter, says as much:

> "You don't need to have been in this job for very long before you can spot the difference between a personalised cover letter and a copy-pasted cover letter a mile off. That's a shame, as there are some candidates who certainly have the skills for the job, but their cover letter lets them down. It just screams lack of interest. On the other hand, if it's clear the candidate has taken the time to get to know the organisation they are applying, I guarantee you that the recruiter

| will be interested."

WRITING THE LETTER

With all of this information in mind, now is the time to start writing your letter. A cover letter has a specific structure that must be respected; if you do not follow it, your chances of success will be significantly reduced. Moreover, employers have a limited amount of time to spend on each application, so if your letter is too long – on no account should it take up more than one side of A4 paper – or does not get straight to the point, they will waste no time moving on to a letter that does.

The heading

This extremely formalised section will allow you to get right into writing your letter without having to stare at a blank page for half an hour. It gives the recruiter the factual information that they need.

- Your contact details: in the upper right corner, put your full name, your address, your phone number and your email address. This information will allow the employer to contact you easily without having to search for your contact details. This may seem like a minor detail, but it is extremely important that you are easy to contact.

- The employer's contact details: in the upper left corner, underneath your personal information, write the contact details of both the business and (if you know them, of course) the recruiter. Write "Dear Sir/Madam" (or their name, if you know it) underneath. This can be useful if the letter is opened by someone other than the person you are writing to. Therefore, it does not matter if you repeat the information already on the envelope.
- The date of sending: write the date in full under the employer's contact details, but above "Dear Sir/Madam". For example: "13th March 2017".
- The subject of your letter: underneath "Dear Sir/Madam" you should write the name of the job you are applying to, based on the advert reference, if there is one. Write it as follows: "RE: (reference)"

The introduction

As its name indicates, this part is used to establish contact with the employer without going right into why you should get the job. It is made up of two parts: the salutation and the opening paragraph.

First, state who you are writing to. If you do not know exactly who this is, use "Dear Sir/Madam". If you know the name of the person in charge of recruitment, write "Dear Mr ..." for a man or "Dear Ms ..." for a woman. However, if you know the job title of the person you are writing to, then write something like "Dear Hiring Manager" or "Dear Human Resources Director". Do not forget to put a comma after your salutation.

Next, start a new line (leaving a space) and begin your letter. The first paragraph should be no more than a few lines long and answer the following question: "Why is the employer receiving your application?" You can therefore begin by briefly mentioning the job advert and where you saw it, and stating when you are ready to start.

The main body of the letter

The main body of the letter should answer three specific questions to pique the recruiter's interest. These three questions correspond to the three parts which normally make up a cover letter.

- **Who are you and why are you suitable for this job?** This is the part where you have to explain why this job and company interest you in particular. Do not forget about the employer and focus too much on the job. Use the information that you have already gathered to develop your argument. The employer must be able to see that you have understood what the job you are applying for consists of. Basically, you have to show that you are in your element. For this part, it is also highly recommended to use the advert as a reference, highlighting the essential points and explaining why they motivate you. A good way to start off could be:

> "I am currently looking for a job as a … in the … sector. I have always wanted a career as a … and I am sure that my experience in … will be a great asset to your business. I am very enthusiastic at the thought of working for a growing, innovative company like …, and I believe that I have all the skills that you are looking for."

This is just a generic example – try to find your own way of introducing things. Do not forget that the most important thing is to personalise your letter as much as possible.

- **How do your skills match what the company is looking for?** This section is dedicated to your experience, to show why you are suited to this position. As a result, it is important to select the most appropriate parts of your CV for the job you are applying for and turn them into arguments to make you stand out from the other candidates. Even if you are applying for a job that is completely different from anything you have done before, try to highlight the qualities and the skills that you have developed and that are also relevant to this new job. What may seem to you to be a weak point can sometimes be transformed into a strength that will allow you to stand out from the crowd. The aim is to therefore highlight the value of your experience to the employer.

This is the most important part of the cover letter, and as such it can be as long as ten to fifteen lines. It is therefore advisable to break it up into two or three coherent paragraphs instead of having one big block of text. Moreover, this will help you to structure your ideas and make it easier for the recruiter to read.

- **Why are you the ideal candidate?** This paragraph is your conclusion: it summarises and brings together the elements that you developed above. It rounds off the letter by showing that you are a good fit for both the job and the organisation's culture. Ideally, you should seem like the obvious choice after the employer has finished reading your application.

Some polite closing phrases

Finish your letter by saying that you remain at the employer's disposal for any queries that they may have about you. Use a simple, classic politeness formula like "Thank you for your time and consideration. I look forward to meeting you to discuss my application further", and sign off with "Yours sincerely" (if you know the name of the person you are writing to) or "Yours faithfully" if you do not. Then all you have to do is sign at the bottom of the page and indicate your name and surname if you are applying by email.

SENDING YOUR APPLICATION

The way you should send your application is always indicated in the job advert. You will be asked to apply either by email or by post. However, you will often be given the choice between the two possibilities. In this case, send your application by post. Employers receive countless emails: your application will be less likely to get drowned in a sea of CVs if you send it by the post.

AN IRRITATING OVERSIGHT

If you are applying by email, make sure you avoid the classic error that we have all already made at least once: double-check that you have definitely attached your cover letter and your CV. Although this may not be anything to worry about in a private context, it can have disastrous consequences for your application: you will either not realise that you have forgotten and the employer will not even look at your CV, or be forced to send it in another email, which will limit the damage but will not completely erase the impression of negligence that you have probably given of yourself.

TOP TIPS

- Use the appropriate jargon for the sector you are applying to. This will reinforce the personalised aspect of your cover letter even more. Obviously, try not to make things too complicated or specialised. The aim is to imply that you have the experience for the job without overwhelming the employer with technical terms.
- Make yourself stand out from the other candidates with some originality. A cover letter may be a relatively conventional document but, depending on the job and the employer, try to judge if some creativity could play in your favour. This spark of originality could be a passion, an unusual experience or a very personal way of presenting things. In any case, avoid clichés. The employer has to feel that your letter is not a carbon copy of the dozens of other applications that they have already received.
- Proofread. Reread your cover letter several times with painstaking attention to detail. If

spelling is not your strong point, ask a friend or family member to reread it for you. No matter the job or sector that you are applying for, spelling mistakes always give a bad impression.

- Use short sentences. If you want to make your letter as clear as possible, avoid long sentences. The recruiter should be able to understand the content of your letter at a glance. On no account should they have to reread an unclear passage because of a complex sentence. However, be careful not to go overboard: the aim is to write a clear cover letter, not a list.
- Be honest about your skills. Obviously, you have to paint yourself in the best possible light, but lying and inventing elements to make your application look better will come back to bite you during the interview or later on.
- Be enthusiastic. The tone of your letter should convey your motivation, without giving the impression that you are overconfident: this can be seen as arrogance or boasting by the employer.
- Maintain your dignity. Do not grovel. Playing on pity will not work.
- Avoid repeating yourself. There is no point returning to something that you have already

gone over or expressing it again in a different manner. You only have one side of A4: you need to make the most of the space that you have! Make sure your letter is written accordingly.

- Your sentences should always be positive. Reword all negative phrases if there are any. This may seem trivial, but negative sentences have a damaging effect on the impression given by your letter.
- Use a simple layout. Although your content should be a little more original, play it safe when it comes to the structure, except maybe if you are applying for a job in the artistic sector. Write in black and use a classic font (Arial, Times New Roman or Calibri). Also, make sure you do not hide the content of your letter with everything around it: it is the most important part of your letter, and it should therefore be as readable as possible.

FAQS

WHAT MAKES AN EMAILED COVER LETTER DIFFERENT FROM ONE SENT BY POST?

When you apply by email, there is no need to type up your cover letter in a Word document and then attach it to the email. You can put your text directly in the email. That means one document less for the recruiter to open, which makes their life easier. However, it is best to type up your letter in a Word document first, and then to copy and paste it into the body of the email. This will prevent any potential disasters, such as accidently sending your email before you have finished it.

As far as content goes, cover letters sent by email should follow the same rules as letters sent by post. However, they both have different forms, since emails have their own conventions that are completely different from those of classic letters. Electronic mail requires less information than classic mail sent by post: you do not need to write a heading, for example. Get straight into the introduction. The first thing to write is therefore "Dear …". You should put your name and contact details at the end of the email. The subject of your cover letter will find its logical place in the subject line of your email.

IS IT A GOOD IDEA TO HANDWRITE YOUR COVER LETTER?

It might be tempting to personalise your letter by writing it by hand, for aesthetic reasons or to stand out even more from the crowd. This sometimes pays off. However, keep in mind that you may give a bad impression of yourself in the digital world of the 21st-century: people might think that you are out of step with modern technology. This is even more important if you are applying for a job in the technology or IT sector.

SHOULD YOU ALWAYS SEND A COVER LETTER WITH YOUR CV?

If it is not specifically asked for in the job advert, you do not need to send a cover letter. However, it will cost you nothing but a bit of time to attach one to your CV, and this will allow you to prove your motivation and interest for the job as soon as the employer receives your application.

WHAT ARGUMENTS SHOULD YOU MAKE WHEN YOU HAVE LITTLE OR NO PROFESSIONAL EXPERIENCE?

When you are just setting out into the world of work, it is obviously difficult to prove your experience. If this is the case, do not lose heart. There are other solutions to highlight your qualities and your skills. The first thing to do is to take a good look at what you have already done and detect any elements that could be useful for the post you are applying to. You may not think so right away, but some of your seemingly trivial experiences may turn out to be very important. Do not just limit yourself to your charity work, internships, or studies; talk about your travels, sporting interests, passions and hobbies as well. Among these elements, try to find the most appropriate skills for the position. The most important thing is to show that, in spite of your lack of professional experience, you are just as capable of taking on the job and its demands as another candidate.

SOME ADVICE FOR YOUR FIRST JOB

Do not explicitly mention your lack of professional experience. The recruiter will notice it themselves from your CV. It is therefore not necessary to draw attention to it: you should try to minimise it, as it could potentially hold back your application.

If, on the other hand, you have the appropriate experience, but not the education, emphasise the former and what you have got out of it, without mentioning your lack of qualifications. This will also be visible from your CV, and adding it to your cover letter may give the recruiter the impression that you are putting yourself down. Try to hide this potential drawback behind the experience, skills and other qualities that you have accumulated.

CAN YOU ADD A TOUCH OF HUMOUR TO YOUR COVER LETTER?

Well, it is true that this guide has constantly emphasised the need to make yourself stand out from the crowd with an original, personalised letter. However, since humour is very subjective, it is a tricky thing to use in a cover letter. In fact, unless you personally know the recruiter, avoid humorous touches. They could go two ways: you could either amuse the employer and grab their attention, or completely discredit yourself in their eyes. If in doubt, it is best to avoid humour.

HOW CAN YOU APPEAR ENTHUSIASTIC WITHOUT COMING ACROSS AS ARROGANT?

In order to stand out from the other candidates, it is important to show your motivation and your enthusiasm for the job and the employer. This is the primary aim of a cover letter. However, be careful your enthusiasm is not seen as arrogance. To avoid this, here is some practical advice:

- Avoid the first person singular as much as you can. In other words, try to minimise the use of the word "I" at the beginning of sentences.
- Never refer to the employer or the job you are applying to in a condescending way. This could happen if, for example, you mention a former, more prestigious employer that you put on a pedestal, even implicitly, compared to the one you are applying to. Of course, you should not play down your experience, but praising a former company or position too much will give the recruiter the impression that you would rather be applying for that job than the one they are offering.
- Avoid inappropriate exclamation marks. If each of your sentences ends with an exclamation mark, the effect you are looking for will be significantly reduced. Use it to highlight one or two particular phrases, no more.
- Do not only talk about yourself and your experience. Remember that the goal is not only to show that you are competent, but also that you are motivated by the job and the employer. Therefore, emphasise the aspects of the job that make you so enthusiastic. The worst thing you can do is make your cover letter into

a page-long boast.

CAN YOU USE THE SAME COVER LETTER FOR EVERY JOB?

All job adverts have their particularities. It is therefore essential to adapt your cover letter to suit them. Even if you find two almost identical adverts for the same job, you still have to adjust your cover letter to fit the two different employers. It is essential to personalise your letter: you should never send an identical letter for two different jobs. Your letters may only have a few minor differences, but it is these very differences which count – you might as well stack all the odds in your favour. The best cover letter is one which conveys your personality while also being tailored to the job advert you are responding to.

SHOULD YOU MENTION THE DISTANCE BETWEEN THE WORKPLACE AND HOME?

Of course, if you live nearby, the address on your cover letter and CV will be enough for the employer to realise that there will be no problem with travel.

If, on the other hand, you live far from the office, it is a good idea to explain why you are looking for a job in the area. For example, if you intend to move to the area where your job is, saying this will play in your favour. This will even make you seem more dedicated. However, if you cannot find an appropriate reason to justify the distance, do not mention it: there is no point in drawing the recruiter's attention to an element which could potentially make them biased against your CV.

OVER TO YOU

You now have all the tools you need to write the perfect cover letter. But, in case you need just a little push to get you started, here is one final list of questions to give you some inspiration if you cannot think what to write.

- Why do I want this job? What is it about it that motivates me the most?
- Why do I want to work for this employer in particular?
- What parts of my career prove that I am qualified for this job?
- What have I got that other candidates do not?
- What is my proudest achievement? Can I use this in my favour?
- Is there a domain in which I particularly excel? If so, should I highlight it?
- Which of my character traits fit this job?
- Are there any other reasons the employer should hire me (distance between work and home, knowledge of a foreign language which could come in handy, etc.)?

<u>**WORK WITH KEY WORDS**</u>

It can be useful to draw up a list of key words by category. Answer these questions, noting which key words come to mind. Next, classify them into groups like "skills", "motivation", "experience", "specific assets", and so on. Whether during the writing or the rereading of your letter, think about consulting these categories again to make sure that you have not forgotten anything. Finally, do not lose heart if you do not get the job. This does not mean that you are incompetent. Keep on applying for jobs – you will get there eventually!

We want to hear from you!
Leave a comment on your online library
and share your favourite books on social media!

IMPROVE YOUR GENERAL KNOWLEDGE

IN A BLINK OF AN EYE !

www.50minutes.com

www.50minutes.com

Ebook EAN: 9782808000215

Paperback EAN: 9782808000222

Legal Deposit: D/2017/12603/438

Cover: © Primento

Digital conception by Primento, the digital partner of publishers.